FIRST CUT

Poems
for Ghosts
in empty tenement windows
I thought
I saw once

by
Stephen J. Golds

Close To The Bone Publishing

Dedicated to
the faces
in the crowd
on the day
I'll hang

Contents

◆

I

II

III

I

Bleeding out while
an ant crawls along
a chain link fence

My Parents Worried

At six years old
chewing bubble gum,
I enjoyed playing
Russian Roulette
with a cap gun.

Knock, Knock

Nothing tastes sweeter
than that last mouthful of whiskey
after fifteen days sober
with a black eye, a broken molar &
a Jehovah's Witness tapping at the door.

A Summer Day Dragging Like

the untied lace of a dirty sneaker.
All the coins in a wishing well
rusted circa 1980.
An old Ford up on bricks,
its engine gone.
I held ocean water
in my cupped palms once
& saw only the sky there,
no gods.

I Carry

The cemetery inside me.
Too often I visit it to loiter among
the graves, placing my hands
on the too cold stones,
scraping away the moss that's
grown over the important parts.
Drunkenly I mourn, knowing
things that are dead,
stay dead.
And maybe
that's for the best.

A Broken Record Playing to an Empty Room

It's when I'm alone
in my own apartment, my own bed that
I think about her most and I'm alone
in my own apartment, my own bed a lot recently. Too much.

Leaving for work while darkness still lingers in the sky,
Occasionally, I glance back into the hallway and
catch a glimpse of her there like a shadow passing
across the walls, a ghost in a photograph.

Does the love we might have had
haunt the empty rooms of her apartment
as it drags itself around the floorboards of mine
leaving behind a bitter scent that stings the eyes?

When she cleans the dishes in the kitchen sink,
feels the hot water over her hands does the memory of us
fucking there ever flash through her mind, a momentary
blinding stroke of lightning in the skyline of that deserted city?

The couch too, when she's sat there watching tv
with the newest one, the one that isn't anything
like me, does she feel me there too?
Inside her again like a tear in the fabric of the seat,
or a dark stain on the cushions that she can't scrub out?

When she places the needle down on an old record,
let's the music we shared crowd the air from that
cheap record player and sways slowly in her bedroom
does she remember that I was the one

7

who taught her
how to
really
dance?

Dread

The gut ache that doesn't ease,
the dishes unwashed in the sink,
the laundry making murder
shapes on a sticky floor.
Windows left open for the rain.
The fever in the night,
all too black & too loud.
The telephone unrung.
The bills sealed by the front door.
Waiting on tomorrow
like it's the goddamned
firing squad.

Unbalanced

When I was 8 years old
I tried to hang myself
from my cabin bed
with a belt

because all of
my broken toys
wouldn't fit
in the toy box.

When I was 34,
I tried again
for the same
reasons.

She was Always Quicker

Like the child discarding the toy
then becoming distraught when another child
picks it up to play with it,

I thought as I dialed, listening
to the dial tone, wondering if
I should hang up but didn't.

She'd already blocked my number &
I wished like hell
I'd just hung up.

That 2 a.m. Drunken Telephone Call

Another one for the books.
For the first aid kit
kept under the sink.

And with empty hands,
I walk the tide and
pick at drifting trash.

There are holes here
for the dead. A box full
of buttons but
no needle and no thread.

Another one for the bar
with the wonky stool and
the whiskey shots after
the last train before last call.

And it's always
the last call.

An Ode to The Japanese Marilyn Monroe

When I first met you in that darkened bar,
I thought you were
a Japanese Marilyn Monroe.
Your lips mouthed sex,
your eyes whispered laugher and
your hair spoke dyed
ash blonde electricity.
Sex and beauty were always
your currencies and
you almost bankrupted me.

Towards the end
we were just two bodies
slow dancing in the dark and
stabbing each other
to death
in a damp attic.
You killed me
many times
but you always
knew how to do that best.

A friend got to showing me
your wedding photo the other night.
And perhaps I caught your eyes
for the final time in that darkened bar.
But this time
you were wearing the long ivory dress
of a proud bride,
not the short skirt and
easy smile
of an easy party girl.

I saw the guy stood crookedly
next to you in a cheap suit,
who seemed a poor imitation of me.
I wondered
if that was deliberate
on your part
but I doubted it.
I looked at the woman
in the photograph and
I still saw the Japanese Marilyn Monroe.

I saw the woman
who tossed the diamond necklace
I'd bought her off
a downtown Hanoi hotel balcony
into the deep blue
of a swimming pool below.
Who kissed me softly
on the face in a back-alley clap clinic
after a Friday lunch and
after six shades of roses.

I saw the woman
who had sent me images of her
tits, pussy and then shallow self harms, and
who made all those suicide late night calls.
I saw the woman
who had made me breathless
with any number of injuries that I've come to
avoid acknowledging like a war-torn vet.
You were my Okinawa,
my Viet Nam, my Iraq and my Somme.

I saw the woman
who had laughed at the most
unsociable of times, and
the woman who'd gone to her knees
in the most unlikely of locales.
Who loved to fuck
everywhere but between sheets.
Who'd worn my shirts around the apartment
and my sunglasses swaying in the park and
who had lied about being on birth control.

I always imagined
seeing your wedding photograph
would bring back
a lot of the undead and unhealed,
but I just gulped at my warm beer and
wondered if the guy stood haphazardly
next to you knew exactly
what he was getting himself into.
Marilyn Monroe had been
a very sad and a very sick woman after all.

The Way This Blood Feels on My Fingers Tonight

I forget how long it's been sometimes, Darling.

The last time I saw you
you fled into an empty night
screaming at me you were going to throw yourself
from the top of an apartment building.
We had both laughed but
our laughs were different then,
weren't they, Darling?

The time we argued,
I can't remember what about now,
you gave yourself to the traffic.
I'd gone after you,
horns blaring and lights screaming,
flashes in the night.
Following you into that damp darkness, Darling.

And yes, there were all the times
you shared yourself with others,
and smiled with lips like Babylon.
Little deceits grown grotesque.
And I took you back
I always took you
back, Darling.

I remember the way your hair
felt underneath my fingertips,
but tonight I'm running
my fingers over these ripened tight scars
that you left behind when you left here.
Jagged glass lovers,
that we were, Darling.

You were married when I met you,
we broke each other's vows like porcelain.
We both lied together while
we lay together.
But things have a habit of ending
the way they started
don't they, Darling?

I forget how long it's been sometimes, Darling.

The Coffee Doesn't Taste the Way It Did Before

The mug has a chip on its lip
and the music that flows from the old speakers
leaks stilted down the wood paneled walls.

The black and white
photographs are still hanging there
but I sit here alone now.

I heard you'd got engaged.
I drink from the mug,
the tip of my tongue
touches the rough, broken porcelain.

The coffee doesn't taste the way it did before.
I'll stand up, unknown, uninvited and unloved.
I'll pay and I'll leave.
I'll not come back here again

23 Days Since

I last
saw your face &
through the blank dusty space
of your apartment door
you screamed at me

you loved me no more,
you were calling the cops &
I was fucking crazy,

when I said
I'd made a mistake &
I loved you still.

You had a new lover there already,
(patiently prepared or newly made)
hiding behind your back.
23 days after
3 years of
knowing only us.

When I finally sobered
the next evening
I wondered
who was really
fucking crazy
you or I?

II

Sometimes
love is
like footsteps in
an empty, damp night

Diet

Stepping naked
onto the scales
after a shower
this morning,

the needle
informed me
I had lost 5kg.

It's as though you were
a weight of muscle
wasted and gone.

It is said
the human soul
weighs 21 grams,

I wonder what else
was ripped away from me
the day I kicked you out.

Uninhabited

Palsied hands on a door
too white in this
early morning fog.

Empty bottles &
words like shards
of broken things.

Wearing the dull
costume of a part never
intended to be played.

Unable to recall
the words said,
though these scars remain.

Visiting Hours

Sitting across
from someone

you love
in a
mental hospital,

talking about
the weather
is the
craziest thing
of all.

Recycle

I go to restaurants
and bars we went.
Sit there at an empty table,
an empty glass in my empty hand.
Wanted to remember how it was
but I can't.
I've tried.
Nothing comes.

I ride the subway around the city.
Always end at the beginning.
No way out.
Wanted to get away,
see something new
but I can't.
I've tried.
Nothing comes.

I lay in the beds of others
while they breath out
softly into an unmoving night.
My eyes never close. Just darkness.
Wanted to love
but I can't.
I've tried.
Nothing comes.

There's pain, a bright blade
in the hollowness of my guts.
Unremovable. Unremitting.
Unrequited.
Wanted to hate
but I can't.
I've tried.
Nothing comes.

I'd like to cry or laugh.
Baptisms for ghosts.
Imagine it would be a relief.
All things brought anew.
Wanted to grieve, move on
but I can't.
I've tried.
Nothing comes.

I question
which one of us is dead?
Who died on that humid summer day?
Cutthroat and tongue tied.
Wanted to know
but I can't.
I've tried.
Nothing comes.

For a Girl Called Clarissa Who Has a Different Name Really

You didn't count to 10,
I thought that was unfair.
When you gunned me down,
I lay there shocked and awed.
Bled out,
bullet riddled and gun shy.
I didn't know because you never told me
that we were playing for keeps, Clarissa.

7/11

My love something
like the fly
against the storefront
glass until death.
She is gone.

Poteen

The newest one,
she doesn't talk about you,
doesn't ask about you.
Ever.
The same way
all the new ones are
about the old ones, I suppose.

But last Thursday night
walking home
drunk together
she surprised us both
by asking me to compare you
to something.
Anything.

I didn't know what to say,
both honesty & deceit
were a wild animal
bloody, snarling in a bear trap.
We walked until the sounds
of our footsteps were almost deafening
& then finally

I said you, the older one, the one before
was like the bottle of bittersweet Poteen I drank
when I was twenty-four, depressed and crazy.
She asked me why? I said it made me very ill,
put me in the hospital &
I never drank the stuff again.
Never forgot about it either.

Then she, the newest one,
asked me to compare her too and
I said she was a smooth whisky highball.
Underneath the streetlamps, her face fell slightly.
A fleeting sadness flashed across her face like a shadow.
I didn't know why then.
And almost a month later I still don't.

My Grandfather's

shocked blue face
in the morgue
hours after death
taught me everything
I ever needed to know.

Backpacker

She showed me the blisters
on the heels of her feet.
Told me she swam in the river Ganges.
I asked her if that was the river of the dead?
She grinned, drank from my bottle & said
she hoped so, otherwise
what would have been the fucking point?

Broken Windows

Pink smiles sketched into naked flesh,
self consciously massaged in lamp light.
A night as haunted as a house of broken windows –
she asks me to go buy more wine.
I say yeah okay and start to get dressed.
Never having liked wine very much at all.

Love

She slumped drunkenly
against the bar,
slipped the high heel
from her foot,

smacked the
other girl
over the back
of the scalp with it.

Screaming I was her man.
The other girl screamed too,
something ethereal &
the blood flowed hot.

I thought as I stared,
I wanted to marry
the woman with
only one shoe.

Early Hours

Sitting on my apartment balcony,
drinking whiskey coffee
at 2:45,
watching the city
stirring in its sleep.

The young woman across the way
undressed, naked, standing in a
yellow window.

I look away, light a cigarette,
feeling too depressed and alone
to really see anything at all.

Questions Over an Empty Grave

The woman who called me on my cellphone
to wish me a happy day before
I pushed myself into the rush hour subway
wasn't the one
I had hoped it would be.
You, I mean. You.

The woman who knocked on my door at 1 a.m.
with a wicked smile &
a gift of something she thought
I wanted, needed, no,
she just wasn't you either.

And that's the way I've been thinking...
I'd like to think
you're painfully thinking
of me
this painful way I'm thinking
of you.

But, I know. I know
you've already washed me
away with
last night's date &
this morning's shampoo.

What is this bloody mess
I'm grasping with in my stained hands,
this septic wound coined Love when
I'm the only one left
holding the damned, poisoned thing?

You said you'd go with me
into that black place, but
the darkness always scared you and
I let go of your hand
somewhere months back.
I didn't even realize you were gone.
Were you really even here to begin with?

You said I need to change but tell me
where is the success, the victory
in changes made and problems fixed,
when they're improvements made alone &
birthed from a death like this?

What are the true weight of
a lover's kisses
in the humidity of the
rain drenched night
when they aren't yours
on my sensitive flesh?

What is the meaning of sex if
I'm no longer moving inside you?
It's something boiled down to
a self congratulatory act
of malice that leaves me
spinning records with ghosts
isn't it?

And finally, finally,
what good is being happy
if it's being happy
without you
now that you're just another
dull ache that
I carry around
in my guts?
You, I mean. You.

All the Unanswered Things

Love is subway stations
out of the town you grew up in
and love is the dials on the washing machine in the laundromat
when you've used the last of your change on the coke machine.

Love is the rabid spotted dog
that barks, refuses to sit
and love is the black alley cat grinning
after you've trodden in its shit.

Love is the silver pocket watch
from the flea market in London that stopped at 12:06
and love is the crumpled paper airplane
in the classroom wastepaper basket.

Love is that moisture on your face
when you're without tissues
and love is trying to smile at yourself in the
mirror on a Monday morning before work.

Love is the movie bank heist gone wrong
with a crew full of psychopaths and bad acting
and love is the overweight librarian
without her reading glasses.

Love is going to sleep
not dreading tomorrow
and love is something that
I am thinking about now
it's too late.
You're gone.

With All the Love that Wasn't Enough

It's hard for me to sleep knowing
you're in someone else's bed tonight,

being all too painfully aware we share
the same night, the same darkness

but that's
all now.

III

Lose color
a picture in feverish light
Fade out
A screen projected
fallen to black
Be gone
take these aching wounds
with

The Mornings After

Before in the well worn silence
of my kitchen & something
that might have been love,

coffee black like your hair
& your eyes. Hot like we were,
percolating, boiling.

Scolding, the kind that leave
behind those fleshy, itchy reminders
of something
that might have been love.

Lips

Of all the people
who have spoken
my name
I think it was you
who said it best.
But now it's silent here,
no one calls out for me.
I am alone and
your lying lips
know the shape of another.

It's Time to Go Home

There's a rent dodging fool
called Love in my heart with a
loaded .38 in his fist &
a bullet-riddled target in sight but
the last train is already at the final station.
The lights snap off one by one,
darkness comes down like a curtain of cold.
I can't remember where the fuck I left my coat.

OCD Dinner Date

I notice the finger smudges on the surface of the table.
Listening to the buzzing fan circulating the dusty air.

A water stain a smirk on a fork.
Counting in my head. Counting in my head.

Someone on a table across the way snorts and sniffs.
Bloody crucifixes. Counting. Counting.

Lost my appetite but will grin through dinner
until the check comes, go home and shower.

The Old Hospital on The Hill

My mother worked there nights as a nurse and
in the summer time the patients
would all be draped in starched white
wandering around the yellowed lawns.
Lost in numb familiarity.

We would sneak onto the grounds
to watch them.
One of the older kids
said he'd fucked one of the crazy women.
I laughed, pretending to smoke a cigarette.

The last time there, a fat tattooed man
with purple facial scars chased us away
screaming "you no good cunt!" like a scratched CD.
Even at eleven years old I knew
I was running from something that was a part of me.

Not So Long Ago

My soul might've been beautiful once but
I sold it cheap to a woman
pretending to be everything
I thought I wanted.

She later discarded it
with a used condom
in a bathroom stall
on a beach in Guam.

She never wrote that
in the postcard of course and
I doubt she
even used a rubber.

Something Like a Self-fulfilling Prophecy

I read once that the Native American Navajo tribe
believed those who ate and laughed with
loved ones
died well.

Those that ate in silence,
alone,
died badly.

I think about that often
when I get up to pay the check,
glancing quickly at the
empty seat opposite me.

Start of a Weekend

I watch a once beautiful woman dancing
alone to Zumba music in her kitchen.
She has a quiet satisfaction in her face
I am quite sure I'll never know again.

I quickly wipe away a tear
that caught me by surprise.
Attempting something like a smile,
I press the doorbell to pick up our daughters.
The music stops and I wait.

Beach Front Motel

A burial at sea, playing
Russian Roulette
with kamikaze memories.
Drunk on the beach,
didn't know if the tide
was coming in or going out.

My star sign tattoo'd on your skin,
icebreaker for a heart-breaker.
A 24-hour Band-Aid.
Beach girl who couldn't swim
in a sports bra, dress & sneakers.

Little traumas worn on our sleeves,
& in our hair like sand.
Poured my beer into the Pacific
when you said you hated drink.
A one night showing - movie matinee.

Came to share my darkness,
along that boardwalk
in that September Okinawa rain.
Just for a little while
and that was all right.

In a motel with a blocked toilet,
your hands on my face,
the moonlight on yours,
I thought I glimpsed
all the ones before and
all the ones to come.

After, we examine each other's
scars, listening to the surf.
You said you'd never
done anything like this before.
I said I might be back
for Christmas vacation.

Both accomplished liars &
that was all right. Waiting
on that sunrise with you.
And it's all right now,
don't worry about me,
I slept on the plane.

After the Procession

Casket's mahogany
too dull,
Lilac's scent
too sick
& the
priest's voice
too droning
in that
church too
small for
what you
meant to me.

Crowd

Describe your rips & scars to me,
I'll tell you mine. Like the blind
touching the faces of strangers & knowing,
then later pushing passed one another on
a darkened subway avoiding eye contact.

I'll Never Forget

Wearing the sneakers my mother had
gotten from a catalogue
smiling on half-price sale for my birthday.

The kids at school sneered, pointed with
fingers like pistols.
Somehow they always knew.

I never wore them again &
Mother kept paying the layaway.

15

Alone in that old house,
it felt the least haunted then.
Smoking my father's cigarettes,
sipping at his whiskey.

knowing I should be at school but
realizing that was just exchanging
one kind of isolation for another.

I'll Give It Your Name

"Right here", I said. "I want your mark on me".
She trembling, holding the straight razor,
couldn't do it, hurt me that way.
It wasn't in her nature, she said.

But she fucked a guy she met
from the internet instead.

Mercy

A damp Sunday afternoon,
walking with my father
through fields.

We found a rabbit
that was blind and deaf,
its fur moved like water
underneath my tiny fingertips.

My father snapped its neck.
The kindest thing, he said.
I was seven years old
and I cried.

My father shook his head at me,
the dead rabbit hanging limp from his fist
like so many words unsaid.

Medicine

The clinic was empty &
the smell of her lingered
over my hands & fingers.

Tinny music left small speakers,
my sneakers dancing alone on pure tiles &
the overweight nurse at the reception desk frowning.

I grinned a little, while I
waited, thinking if anyone
had made me sick,

I was happy
it was
her.

Walking Back to My apartment

She makes me promise.
I spit out the words she wants me to say,
knowing I've broken vows
to God,
the dead and
women
who mattered more than she ever would.

For You, My love

You always said
I only wrote poems about *those bitches*.
So this poem, like this drink
I made just for you.

I would have liked to read it aloud to you
while you lay next to me in bed, the covers pushed down or
over fresh coffee in the morning before work or
on the beach shielding our eyes to an orange sun or
while seated on a bench in a park at midnight or
in the bathroom while I showered, and you brushed your teeth or
on the bus going somewhere we weren't quite sure of yet or
over dinner in a restaurant that had plastic bamboo plants in pots or
holding you in my hands like hot water in the bathtub of
the motel by the train station we used to go on Thursday afternoons.

But you left too abrupt,
blamed me for not giving you enough.
Now
this is a poem for
another
one of those bitches.

I hope you like it.

That Dark Mutt

You awake at 4:30.

An aching darkness like a sucking gut wound.

You know little but you know.

Every letter is a firm rejection.
Every phone call is a dead line.
Every friend is an intruder.
Every lover is a stranger.

You can't read.
You can't write.
You can't fuck.
You can't love.

You glare at the small pills
like pebbles from a childhood
river in your palsied hand and
let them fall down the drain.

You're drained.

You write off the day and
go back to try and sleep in a bed
that feels like a stranger's and
maybe it is.

Sometimes My Grandmother Let Me Play Hooky From Elementary

I didn't like the parking garage at the shopping mall.
My grandmother said that many people
had killed themselves there.

I felt their hands in mine as
we walked back to
her old Ford with the bags of groceries.

Acknowledgments

I would like to acknowledge and say thank you to the magazines where these poems were originally published.

Versification,
Punk Noir,
The NonConformist,
Clay Literary,
The Daily Drunk,
Chronogram Magazine,
Fahmidan Journal,
Poetry Life and Times,
Neuro Logical Magazine,
The Taj Mahal Review,
Unpublishable Zine,
Synchronized Chaos,
The Sock Drawer.

Printed in Great Britain
by Amazon

54218477R00041